BLUEPRINTS FOR A GENOCIDE

Rob Cook

SPUYTEN DUYVIL

New York City

Library of Congress Cataloging-in-Publication Data

Cook, Rob, 1969-
Blueprints for a genocide / Rob Cook.
p. cm.
Poems.
ISBN 978-1-881471-31-8
I. Title.
PS3603.O5756B58 2012
811'.6--dc23
2012025952

blueprints for a genocide

(prologue:
walking back to january)

How the ground repeats
              the dinosaur wreckage
that slogged this far
        through the shale
        evenings.

Buildings gnawing the cold
              with rows of sharp
              ledges.

More compassionate to look inside
              one rice grain
              than to notice in front of you

the woman fondled by her tight
mink clothing.

And though the smell of you
              ignoring her—caught on store
              surveillance—will follow her

to the last shade
              of your intricate loneliness,
        the money that understands
        everything about

you, and the money that understands
nothing,
        will return as well to winter,
                    buried on a windswept
                    dime lost

for the three-hundredth day
                    without work,

the three-hundredth day
                    since the footprints of buildings
                            led only to more
                            footprints.

The ice age chat rooms repeat
                    the tribes of stillness
                    fighting over
                    the maps to the skeleton
                    summer.

Wind destroyed by drapes in the eyes of mastodons.

The moonlight stays
trapped inside
                    a cigarette child groping through
                    the salt storms
                    and tenement blizzards.

How each window is a photograph
of the hominids walking
back to January.

They curse by using the spines
and organelles of a word
            rather than the word itself.

            The gladiators
            of the opinion coliseums

and anonymous mating fortresses

skinning each other

without sound,
without weapons,

and without even a finger's believable warmth.

1.

Looking
for
hope
I
hacked
into
an
unsafe
word
and could not
see
past
the
millions
of
people
stacked
like
cords
of
wood.

Not one teacher said to leave the words alone.

From
the
windows
of

the
champagne
laptops
the
buildings
lurched once
and then stopped.

"We will take away your greed. We will take away your greed."

A song instead of an algorithm.

A song instead of a dollar's terrace-feathered statues.

Crushed into six words
with a million people inside

whose feet made the sound of a strong but unrecognizable weeping.

2.

Those who are mostly people
hold hands
from New York to California.

They no longer have money
to suffocate
out on the hospice prairies
and cardboard grasslands.

Today the children
are made of falling snow

and deep inside their bodies,

among the tunnels
and telephone lines
connecting
all the rooms of the Earth,

the hate speech of football
continues.

A boy and a girl
who survived the stillness of coca-cola
gather the knives thriving
where the mistakes of narcissus
once grew.

The boy fondles and heals the girl
where she's pregnant with an older man's blanket.

On one road sign the sun is shining.
On another less than one bed makes it through the child-long night.

A mother of three carrying a hundred dollars
like a hundred snow angels inside
her aching dress
asks for shelter beneath a sign whose words have fallen
gullibly to the ground.

3.

Listen
to
our
feet
as
they
chant
from
the
bottom
of a
passive but violent
dollar.

Some
of
us
get
disoriented
in
our
words
like
galloping
parts
of
the
night

impaled
on
headlight
beams.

Some
of
us
walk
to
the moon,
the
one
that
is
more
cold
than
the
others,
and
do
not
return.

Some
of
us
hate,
and
there
is
evidence.

We
curse
in
percentages
because
our
shadows
have
fallen
into unmarked holes
in
the
songs
of
heaven.

We
drink
from
where
the
few
look
at
us,
leaving
their
plundered
wells.

We
follow

the
few
who
march
in
perfectly
aligned
columns
to
their
homes
inside
a
gated
stupor
of
zeroes.

The
few
who
sell
their
names
to
the
trees
and
sunflower
decimals
and
sip
from

acorns
and
lakes
of
gas
and
dismantled
rainbows.

We
cough
as
far
as
the
families
of
December
that
poison
the beds
of
those
who
created
us
from
community
halls
operated
by
nuns
half-missing

in
television
sleet.

We
are
the
diminished
grasses
healed
by
insect
nurses.

We
take
our
commandments
from
the
obedient
but
gifted
veal
and
milked
dry
prodigies
during
the
fragile
summer.

We
pollinate
the
crosshairs
of
the
Elliot
Management
Corporation
with
half inch
rallies
and
cloud
settlements
and
the
clean
but
passing
cries
of geese.

We
are the
few.

We
are the
few.

We
puncture

the
towers
of
porcelain
mosquitoes
and
collect
the
trillion
eyes,
the
trillion
diamond
raindrops
clattering
without
sound
to the
hard-blooded
pavement
where,
like
a foot
that
consumes
the
thunder
of
nearby
boot-steps
and
produces
less

livable
space,
we are
encouraged
to
live,
and
to
kidnap
the
closest
shoe,
force
it
to
be
the
same
shade
as
a
dollar
when
it
collects
the
shivering
of
a
child
made
of
leaves

that
turn
yellow
and
reveal,
with
obsolete
references
to
foliage,
the
blood-thin
velocity
of
someone
either
attacking
or
falling.

4.

Without
the
required
three-syllable
demands,
the
people
scatter
like
leaflets
of
shale
and
pharmaceutical
experiments
derived
from
an
apocryphal
kindness.

We
have
continents
of plastic
where
the
slime-papered

gogs
of
Zondor
celebrate
the
community
college
Iliads
with
silicon
picnics
and
ironic
spaceship
summers.

Forks
and
knives
and
faces
at
the
bottom
of
spoons
will
be
tested
for
their
intelligence
in

all
the
directions
of
time
and
dreaming.

We
will
be
kidnapped
from
our
colds
and
cancers
and
downloaded
into
the
wind's
hidden
work
camps.

We
will
be
forced
by
our
own

subsidized
melancholy
to
justify
every
word
we've
ever
carried
from
one
room
of
untelevised
Byron
to
another,
every
word
not
devoted
to
the
seven
minute
marriages
between
melted
athletes
and
famous
lipstick
sadnesses.

We
will
be
encouraged
to
blame
the
flunking
Rimbaud
pageants
on
those
among
us
with
shadows
that
do
not
burn.

The
latest
millisecond's
judgment
will
infiltrate
the
selves
we
bookmarked
as

"memories
from
granddad"
back
when
the self
was
eliminated
by children
in their
after
school
theaters
of
"kill
the
boy
with
the
ball"
while
the
trojan
cheerleaders
boiled
and
screamed
and
made
their
bodies
smile
in
formation.

5.

Today
the
wind
seemed
like
a
distorted
person
kicked
into
Chinese
storage.

Today
the
leaves
stiffened
on
their
branches
and
the
snow
fell
in
emergencies
of
unexpected

gulags.

Today
men
paid
for
the
morning's
blameless
arrival
with
money
as
it
bled
to
death
in
their
hands.

Today
the sun
shorted out
and
barely
perceptible
sticks
of
consciousness
grew
in
long

marches
from
interior
computer
dungeons.

Today
the
trees
drifted
away.

Today
the
trees
drifted
the
distance
of
one
leaf
and
disappeared.

Today
men
traded
hard
fear
from
their
god-stained
shirts

in
the
fjords
of
the
stock
exchange.

Today
the
members
of
the
female
storm
movements
and
their
hands
taller
than
the
shadows
of
men
revealed
the
earliest
words
of
their
mostly
i-phone

infants
and
paid
for
them
to
stay
at
ten
months
old
with
ten
months
of
crazy
for
the
crowds
funding.

Today
we
drank
water
cut
with
scissors
from
a
patch
of
cloth

as
it
either
screamed
or
suggested,
in
uncharted
colors,
how
that
scream
would
survive.

Today
we
no
longer
heard
the
pennies
biting
and
trading
prayers
with
each
other
at
the
bottom
of

our
bone-clap
pockets.

Today
the
air
fell
imperceptibly
to
the
ground
and
every
person
named
after
a
numeral
was
eliminated
from
the
page
whose
wendigos
cried
inside
the
wind
and
the
icicle

mangers
and
the
crowded
wilderness
of
thanksgiving.

Today
we
heard
and
saw
and
smelled
and
fought
amongst
ourselves
in
the
panic
of
another
dimension's
visigoths
arriving
with
spring's
viral
mountains.

Today
we
fell
into
an
active
sleep
tracing
snow
after
snow
after
snow
(also
the
snow
that
wronged
us)
and
offered
our
illegal
bodies
as
shelter
to
the
frightened
but
not-yet-proven
chunks
of
wolves.

6.

A
boy
tries
to
turn
the
page.

He
picks
up
the
pieces
when
the
less
than
one
second
deep
media
commands,
"Pick
up
the
pieces!"

He

picks
up
the
pieces
that
are
the
dung
of
an
uncleaned
cupboard's
dust
vertebrates.

Another
boy
who
is
a
tormented
sack
of
gourds
and
radishes
eats
nothing
but
salad
from
the
Monsanto

Family
Restaurant,
a
triangle
structure
near
a
traffic light
no one
remembers,
in
a
town
removed
from
every
encyclopedia.

"He
sure
brings
his
gourds
and radishes
to
the
table,"
a
network
saturated
social
worker
says,

believing
she's
outside
the
box.

The
churches
of
agent
tangerine
sue
the
children
whenever
they
get
sick
with
escape
tunnels
or
non-FDA-approved
cancer
or
sleep
that
evolved
from
grammar
school
innovations.

The
critics
who
shun
any
piece
of
writing
louder
than
a
Latin
comma
or
an
allusion
to
a
labyrinth
hero's
Greek
silences
tell
the
child
not
to
be
"in
the
face
of
the

more
accomplished
Audens"
or
"rough
around
the
edges
of
the
learned
crawdad
tides."

If
the
boy
cannot
be
polite
when
he's
infected
by
a plate's
vegetation,
if
he
cannot
be
positive
about
his

disfigured
handwriting
and
the
parched
shadows
fondling
his
prayers
and
his
always
active
oxygen
tanks,
he
will
not
be
admitted
to
the
graduate
level
bacterial
famines.

The
critic
and
the
literary
agent

and
the
editor
and
the
marketing
executive
and
the
broadcasters
of
foreclosed
tent
families
talk
always
about
"the
end
of
the
day,
the
end
of
the
day,
the
end
of
the
day."

This
is
how
they
destroy
the
world.

The
day
does
not
end
for
the
pork
bladder
that
breaks
down
the
drought
casseroles
and
suburban
flood
loafs
we've
devoured.

The
day
does

not
end
for
the
goats
fleeing
our
always
gasping
stomachs.

The
day
does
not
end
for
the
water
no
one
will
even
whisper
about.

If
you
tell
anyone
at
the
end

of
the
world
that
the
day
does
not
end,
they
will
laugh
at
you
until
they
break
and
then
lock
you
without
a
name
or
a
past
in
the
room
where
Joyce
Kilmer

makes
up
little
lung
noises
to
heal
the
trees
butchered
in
each
line
of
uncomplicated
autumn.

The
boy
puts
his
ear
to
the
wall's
notebook
paper
and
listens
to
the
trees
following
him

home

in

the

other,

remote

consciousness

taken

away

in

the

unharvested

family

restaurant

by

its

busboys

and

waitresses

and

napkin

collection

professionals

working

a

hundred

hours

a

week

in

a

mocked,

already

depleted

currency.

7.

Today the owner of a paper airplane
gets caught on looking glass surveillance
stealing a broom
to sweep the clouds back into his head.

He wades up to his hairline
in the mirror's bone currents
and tidal bruises—

(what happens when a mirror shatters
into unsustainable numbers
of life shards).

"I don't have enough days inside my hand,"
he says, trying to share his pulse
with a knife,

the seahorses leaking from the glare
trapped in its eye.

*

The new Viagra spelling
plotted across the kindergarten
magazine's cosmetic shine
does not tell us:

today it's cold
because no one let
the exterminator indoors.

*

A poet—a cauliflower pervert—
describes the extinctions
necessary for spring:

"If it's a pile of pages you've written,
it will die," the poet says.

"Spring is a vulgar simplicity," she continues.

She doesn't know
that silence is the new transgression.

She chastises the chairs anyway,
for flaunting
where they've been
touched.

Without form.

Not even a moth's narrative.

A softness that turns to diabetes.
Chair after chair.

A treaty against their own explorations.

*

A tsunami filmmaker
writes that it stays cold
when the post-alcohol crowd
abandons Gary Fallout

and his hyphenation freak-gap,
especially how to build one,
also his word for *fuck*.

Not offensive, but deserted.
Not religious, but abandoned.

No birds this far into the mornings
of cloudy red urine,
just the notes of a building
that closed its eyes:
a season, a laceration really, not yet
named in the skyline.

*

"I want to write words that hide the people,"
the poet says
from her retreating beds of rain.

(extortions of people shaped like lyric *w*'s)

(prepositions and the dishonest way a person comes closer)

"I want to sit by the glaciers inside a dollar bill
and command its photosynthesis."

"I want to live with people who grow
shoes instead of food."

She blushes and calls her disturbance a haiku.

And the spring morning—
this time only because she says
it's spring.

8.

(television storm patterns)

High possibility of another
late afternoon city.
A decline in the survival rates
of prepaid smiles.

Early tonight: winds
at the velocity of mountains
drifting deeper inside a goshawk.

A documentary's worth of live lightning static expected
from New York to the ends of the time zone.

Late night lows around twenty
years old or the desperation passed
between black-eyed susans

(temperatures too silent to be found).

And for the morning commute,
watch for thunder lost
on interstate 80 west of Denville—

cleaned-up sky expected
by the time swarm traffic reaches
its packed consensus.

Neighborhoods without books or silence
will heat up indefinitely.

Solar flu predicted for those closest
to the beginning of another
false autumn.

Warm snow at the back of the throat.

(And stay tuned for the pneumonia concerts)

And for the weekend, mostly hatred
enhanced by clouds,
a warning against storm spending
to bring a husband's eyes
back from the clock that melted years ago,

when the minutes still moved
like the freckles on a woman's body.

Rain with no other direction.

No more whispering scheduled
on the radar that warns
of adultery and self-loathing

and the electronic daybreak of children
approaching from the south
in anxious green masses.

9.

storm factories (three variations)

a.

I work inside a box,

no counted hours,
no music,

no promise of a wage

except that I grow in minor
disturbances
of sun

and smelted nickels

with each
cloud unwrapped

b.

Cut, fold
lift

inside the
pouring

box, half a spring

dollar for each
cloud carried

and shipped

each cloud attached
to its proper
color

its form numbered
according

to frequency and angle
of crop

invasion

c.

Inside the box
darken

two families drying

on the haunches
of a forklift—

two families
that begin:

Our young
planted
in the iron grass.

Two families
assigned to each cloud
exhumed—

grownups that sometimes end

the way, from an irritation
inside one's
clothes,

wage clocks feel ruined after rain.

10.

It
is
time
to
clean
the
feathers
from
the
clock,
the
pasteurized
bones
from
the
caves
in
each
minute.

The
mirage
pundits,
whose
words
move
quicker
now,

like
a cobra
with
its
poisonous
monsoon
patterns
deployed,
call
each
lump
of
excrement
a
feather
even
after
they
watched
but
did
not
report
on
the
last
flock
as
it
disappeared
into
the
unknown

horizons
of
a
screensaver
that
belonged
to
a
man
of
fast
food
flesh
named
Chester.

"We
are
the
ninety
nine
percent,"
say
the
chat
room
fondlers
and
the
aspiring
haters
and
the

baby
pushers
and
the
inventors
of clichés
and
the
gun
perverts
and
the
therapeutic
hitmen
and
the
redundant
desk
farmers
and
the
hour
long
pastors
and
the
terminally
beautiful
pharmaceutical
dates
and the
owners
of car surgery

centers
and the
obsolete
pilgrims
who
destroy
the
land
with
their
unending
families.

"We
are
the
ninety
nine
percent,"
each
not
yet
discovered
person
cries
from
the
unmonitored
comment
coliseums.

They
marched

among
the
floods
of
humans.

They
marched
from
one
scrap
of
food
to
a
weaker
scrap
of
food.

They
marched
and
at
the
end
of
that
day
so
many
mention,
if

only
by
reflex,
their
feet
gnashed
at
each
other
and
each
person
was
devoured
by
his
or
her
own
hands
fingers
lungs
heart
and
the
shadows
unknowingly
gathered
and stacked
since
birth,
like
a grasshopper's

kindling.

There
are
more
bacteria
in
one
human
body
than
there
are
humans
on
the
planet
Earth.

"We
are
holes
waiting
to
be
emptied,"
said
the
one
true
life
form
among

us.

The
ninety
nine
percent
buried
him
before
he
found
a
name
that
could
be
remembered.

The
ninety
nine
percent
recorded
his
body
from
each
town
and
left
his
carapace
of

arthritic

halos

in

a

clock

where

no

one

had

time

to

look

or

search

or

smell

the

body

as it

broke

down

into

more

and

more

clocks

whose

feathers

could

be

heard

only

from

certain
painful
shrieks
of
wind
where
so
many
people
gathered,
movement
of
any
kind
was
no
longer
permitted
or
valued
or
even
possible.

11.

I'm
building
a
fort
on
the
surface
of
a quarter.

Everyone
is
welcome
here.

Though
it
is
small,
it
takes
many
edges
and
a
thousand
sightings
of

pine
needles
to
drill
all
the
way
to its
genetic
silver
croplands.

It
is
not
easy
here.

It
is
too
cold
for
the
police
to
find
where
we
are.

We
have

cans
of
food
and
water
without
the
formaldehyde
taste
of
worry.

The
fort
I'm
building
has
work
for
many
shadows.

There
are
always
the
echoes
of
more
mountains
to
hide,
but

no
anti-aging
propaganda
and
the
scaffolding
of
starlight
will
keep
you
safe
and
remembered
at
night.

We
will
have
no
punishable
territories,
and
one
map
on
which
to
write
our
no
longer

coveted
names.

We
will
have
no
trade
agreements
with
pennies
or
dimes
or
nickels
or
the
lamps
that
live
in
the
pages
of
roaming,
desperate
presidents.

We
will
have
nothing
but

the
opening
and
closing
of
our
eyes
to
separate
us
from
the
migrating
wormholes
that
lead
back
to our
false
summer
antibodies
and
their
helicopter
pageants
that remain unfinished.

Nothing
but
paper
seedlings
and
chain-mail

rumors
will
be left
of
us.

And
though
everyone
is
welcome
here,
I
am
still
alone
in
my
fort
with
no
weapons
against
the
benevolent
silence.

I
wake
up
smaller
every
morning

because
I
cannot
see
the
ones
I
love
trying
to
follow
my
broken
windows
to
the
house
of
many
whispering
mansions
I
built
for
them
here
on
the
immolated
hills
and
telescope
plantations

I
found
in
the
pocket
of a
still
breathing
coat
that
didn't
belong
to
anyone.

12.

I've
had
six
years
to
change
the
light
bulbs
in
my
tall
apartment.

They're
like
people
I
used
to
know
and
to
whom
I
no
longer
speak.

I've
had
ten
years
to
set
up
my
dvd
player,
hang
my
curtains,
make
my
bed,
iron
my
sneakers
when
they
weren't yet
parched
with
the kitchen's
linoleum
temperatures.

Today
the
flag
is

leaking
over
my
fire
escape
and
someone
that
won't
go
away
is
knocking
at
my
door
in
a
voice
so
filled
with
snow
it
causes
an
unrepeatable
winter
among
the
fluorescent
tomato
plants.

The
kettle
on
the
stove
is
beginning
to
burn
but
I'm
too
tired
and
the
clothes
I've
worn
since
yesterday
and
the
day
before
also
do
not
want
to
move
from
where

they've
hardened
to
the
already
injured
chair
with
the
books
that
still
need
to
be
read
or
disliked
or
otherwise
emptied.

13.

Today
the
scrap
journalist
of an
unmarked
dressing
room
stopped
scratching
the
sore
on the
back
of her
blouse
responsible
for
the
closeness
of
winter
and
bought,
with a
cement-
filled
dollar,

a pocket
to
hide
her
cold-hearted
clothes
that
could
not
calculate
the
number
of
buttons
and
zippers
she
and her
diamond
slipknot
required
to
survive
the
insides
of a
boutique
mannequin
whose
prices
remain
at
one

minute
of
mostly
evaporated
music
to
feed
the
physically
agreeable
but
otherwise
ravenous,
undeserving
shoes.

14.

The
day
creeps
in
all
its
directions
at
the
speed
of
financial
arousal.

A
man
makes
his
own
children
by
teasing
his
laptop
with
an
accepted
sequence

of
numbers
and
letters,

(the
thistles
and
shell
sounds
of
his
favorite
word)

(or
an
integer
that
never
caused
him
harm)

(at
least
a
word
he
might
recognize
when
threatened)

His
plan:
to
give
his
shadow-
programmed
replicas
a
childhood
among
the
churning
lawns
and
asphalt.

His
plan:
to
bring
back
the
outdoors,
the
basketball
trees
echoing
where
the
children
ended

or
vanished
every
afternoon
near
five
with the
memorization
building's
twenty
minute
playground
and the
mourning
doves
that
no
longer
repeated
the
perimeters
of
hidden
autumns.

Those
who
live
in
the
stolen
millions
say,

mostly
in
numbers,
that
the
crowds
named
after
a
spelling
test
percentage
move
and
think
in
the
slowness
of
uncorrected
milk.

The
lower
beings
who
earn
heavily
edited
paychecks
still
help
each

other
during
the
approaching
obsolescence
of
the
paragraph
and
the
eyeglass
factories
no
longer
thriving
at
those
unreadable
fathoms
where
Ben
Franklin's
insect
burrows
into
a
deleted
hundred
dollar
bill
for
its
grains

and
its
shelter
and
its
charred
vegetation
but
does not
listen
to
the
right
part
of
the
paper
edifice
for its
many
echoing
mandibles.

15.

We
should
scrape
the
scowls
from
the
faces
of
ten story
cologne
models.

Erase
the
granite
nuance
of a
flag
purring
in the
wind
that
watches
everything.

Discredit
the

sentimentality
of a
woman
who
gives
birth
to a
boxcutter
that
shrivels
into
the
shriek
of
still
falling
leaves.

Heal
the
slave
ossuary
in
an otherwise
ignored
dollar
whose
president
won't
stop
deploying
the
cherry

blossoms
he
planted
as
companions.

Trust
the
eyes
and
their
empires
when
the
light
prunes
the
towers
of
their
slowly
bandaged
windows

and
those
behind
them
sipping,
with
an
unearned
happiness,

cups
of
penguin,

bottles
of
trout

(and there is no longer room
to speak without harm).

Talk
anyway,
about
the
freshwater
shark
you
saved
in
some
small
myth
you
told
your
hand
when
the
cracks
in
that

sky

(what we wrongly called birds)

were
late
or
stolen
or
wiped
away
with
the
sweat
of
less
than
one
word.

16.

Last
night
we
were
taken
away
by
a
man
selling
used,
safe
cholera
and
escorted
into
the
catacombs
of
a
penny
where
all
the
replicas
of
the
copper

president
fell
into
the
cold,
gasping
vats
of
morning
mist.

The
man
brought
us
enough
deer
for
more
than
just
a
passing
silence.

He
built
an
entire
sky
with
many
rooms

and
windows
from
the
scabs
he
peeled
off
the
hands
while
they
slept,
already
stolen.

He's
taken
enough
traffic
light
pollen
to
feed
all
the
lines
on
our
maps.

He's
taken

enough
rain
from
the
world
behind
us
to
grow
our
crops
and
eliminate
our
advancing
thirst.

We've
tested
people
for
the
kindness
in
their
shadows
and
recruited
enough
artists
who
can
trace,

without
land
or
lights
at
the
edges
of
the
land,
a
safe
and
unending
food
that
never
suffered.

We
travel
by
thought
and
create
our
sunrises
by
hand
and
plant
ice
cream

trees
wherever
we
feel
the
ground's
pain
in
our
feet.

We
tell
each
other,
though
always
in
different
temperatures,
different
syntactical
palaces,
that
we
will
never
again
have
to
leave
the
extinguished

pine
mountain
kilns
and
freshwater
legacies
of our
infinite
penny
where
we
cried
"no
more
families,
no
more
families"
in the
hard,
one
child
or
less
Lincoln
quiet.

17.

We
repeat
our
groundwater
rage
in the
softest
voice
possible:

chanting footsteps that do not betray each other

We
gather
in
our
middle
class
prayers
of
newspaper
salads
and
cement
steaks
that
shiver.

We
sing,
in
sarcastic
remnants
of
happiness,
god
bless
bank
of
america

once by coplight

twice (this time as one, this time as one)

by violent starlight

18.

The
foreclosures
of
the
body
will
take
place
during
the
unreported
corporate
winter.

There are no more easy messages.

There will be guns praying to other guns.

There will be money that purrs when you touch it.

We will be returned to the cubicles
that have been dug for us,

the hospitals that pass now as spring.

We wait and stand and wait and stand
and it happens, even though the air itself is bleeding:

One corporation offers water from its wounds.

Its message:

There are many mansions—
all of them empty—
inside the overcast dollar
crumpled and drifting like a black hole freighter
in the heavens of your hand.

ROB COOK lives in NYC's
East Village where he co-edits
Skidrow Penthouse. He is the
author of four previous books
and his work has appeared
in Zoland, Caliban, Aufgabe,
The Bitter Oleander, Mudfish,
Pleiades, Harvard Review,
Versal, Rhino, Tarpaulin Sky,
Many Mountains Moving, etc.

S P U Y T E N   D U Y V I L

Meeting Eyes Bindery
Triton
Lithic Scatter

www.ingramcontent.com/pod-product-compliance
Lightning Source LLC
LaVergne TN
LVHW091309080426
835510LV00007B/427